Mosquitoes use their needle-shaped mouths to puncture animals' skin and suck blood. In hot countries they can give people a disease called malaria.

Crane-flies look frightening but the adults are harmless. They lay their eggs in the soil and the young, crane-fly larvae, eat roots. They can damage plants in the garden.

Colorado beetles are pests, too. They eat potato leaves. They do so much damage that if just one is spotted it must be reported.

There are more different kinds of beetle than any other sort of insect. The Goliath beetle from Africa is the heaviest insect of all. It is bigger than a tennis ball.

Not all insects are pests.
Ladybirds (or ladybugs) are bright red
or orange beetles with black spots.
They eat aphids, which suck the
juices out of plants. Ladybirds help
gardeners by doing this.

The bombardier beetle defends itself by
squirting a nasty liquid at its enemies
with a loud pop.

Honey bees do a very important job in the countryside. As they visit flowers they spread the pollen which the flowers need to make seeds.

The bees collect pollen and nectar to feed their young and to make honey. They carry the pollen back to the hive in pouches behind their knees. They tell the other bees where the flowers are by doing a special dance.

There is just one queen in each hive. Her only job is to lay eggs. Worker bees do everything else. They collect food, make cells from wax for the queen's eggs and for storing honey, clean the hive and defend it from enemies.

Like bees, ants live and work together.

Honeydew ants live in the desert in underground nests. The workers collect a sweet liquid given out by insects that feed on plants. They feed it to other ants who swell up like grapes and hang from the ceiling of the nest until the food is needed.

Leaf-cutter ants are farmers. The workers cut leaves into small pieces and take them back to the nest. They use the leaves to grow a fungus which they eat.

Army ants do not build a nest. They march through the forest eating any living creature in their path. They carry their larvae and pupae in their jaws as they march.

Locusts are a kind of grasshopper that live in many countries. When there is plenty of food they breed quickly. In a short time there may be millions. They take off in a huge swarm to search for new food. The swarm makes the sky black. They can eat a farmer's crops in a few hours and may cause a famine for people and animals.

Locusts have strong back legs for jumping. They make a whirring sound by rubbing a special comb on their back legs with their wings.

Male crickets make a loud chirping noise to attract females by rubbing their wings together. Their ears are on their front legs.

The mole cricket lives underground. Its front legs are shaped like spades for digging.

The preying mantis uses its front legs to grasp its prey. Its long green body helps it hide in the leaves.

The flower mantis looks just like a beautiful flower called an orchid. It waits, very still, for its victim to approach. Then, suddenly, it grabs it.

Stick insects and leaf insects are plant eaters. They are camouflaged to hide from hunters like the mantis. They keep still as much as possible and move very slowly so that they do not attract attention. The leaf insect's wings are shaped just like the leaves it sits on. Even the pattern of the veins is the same.

Insect quiz

Now that you have read about insects, how many of these questions can you answer? Look back in the book for help if you need to.

True or false?
1. Insects don't have bones.
2. Young butterflies are called nymphs.
3. Ladybirds (or ladybugs) are beetles.
4. Queen bees make honey.
5. Crickets can hear with their legs.

Is it an insect?

6. Crab

7. Dragonfly

8. Centipede

9. Butterfy

10. Spider

11. Bee

12. Worm

Answers

1. True.
2. False – they are called caterpillars.
3. True.
4. False – the worker bees make the honey, the queen just lays eggs.
5. True.
6. No – crabs have eight legs and a pair of claws.
7. Yes – a dragonfly has six legs and wings.
8. No – this centipede has 30 legs.
9. Yes – a butterfly has 6 legs and wings.
10. No – a spider has 8 legs.
11. Yes – a bee has 6 legs and wings.
12. No – a worm has no legs.